Buddy, let's get this show on the road.

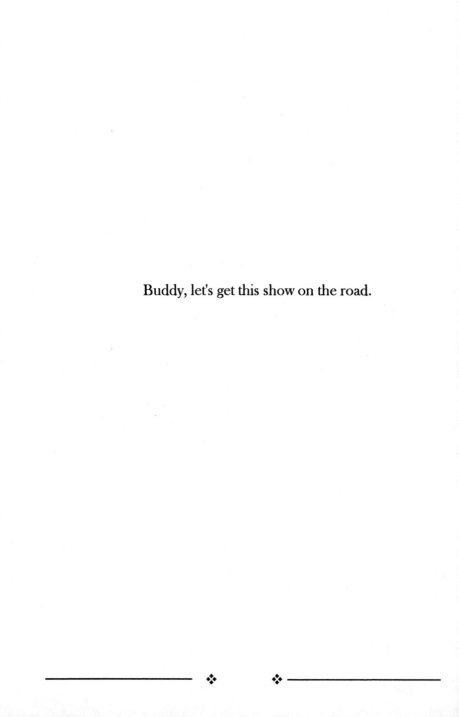

THE ROAD

THAT CARRIED ME HERE

Ray McNiece

Working Lives Series
Bottom Dog Press
Huron, Ohio

ACKNOWLEDGMENTS

These poems have been previously published in the following
journals and magazines: "The Road That Carried Me Here,"
"Love and Fear," and "The Dream Car We Drove West" appeared
as a chapbook published by *Whitefields Press* (Louisville, 1994).
"Homage the Monotony of Summer" and "O Say Can You See?"
appeared in *Poetry on Stage* (Poho Press, Key West) which won
the 1996 Fallot Award for independent publishers. "How Spring
Came and Went" appeared in the *Jamaica Plain Arts News*. "Down
Mt. Greylock" appeared in the *Jamaica Plain Citizen*. "At the
Statue of Mary Dyer" appeared in *Louisville Review* and "I Was
Unemployed in Phoenix" in *Signal*. "This Heron Is" and "That
Blue Spigot Handle" appeared in *Tributaries*. "In the Heron's
Heaving" appeared in *Blue Unicorn*. "In a Field Above the Free-
way" appeared in *Atelier*. "The Definition of Making a Living"
was commissioned by The Labor Studies Program at Wayne State
for the Bernie Firestone Labor Conference, and subsequently
published in *Pudding House*. "The Chagrin Watershed" was com-
missioned by Case Western Reserve University's Historical Sym-
posium. "The Big Easy Sway" appeared in *Desire Street*.

Ohio Arts Council
A STATE AGENCY
THAT SUPPORTS PUBLIC
PROGRAMS IN THE ARTS

Contents

The Road That Carried Me Here

I can still stand up and stretch out
every inch of the last legs
of this past year's tour
of another day another 400 miles and miles of orange barrels
and Jersey barriers and
flat-out hauling ass on the slab at 74.9 MPH,
just under the radar-gun aim,
hueing to the grooves down to the threads of the treads,
leveled off at an altitude of 3 feet above pavement ETA ASAP,
not a day later or a dollar shorter.

So I'm hueing to the grooves down to the threads of the treads,
sailing right on through, sailing right on through
that *HEY STUPID* light waving it's orange flag from the dashboard!
I've got my feet floored on the heatshield
like John Glenn's Mercury re-entry
as America's schizophrenic landscape peels away on either side,
paradise overlaid with a forest of fast-food signs,
one long mono-sodium glutamate boulevard from sea to oily sea.
You can buy yourself a piece of fried American apple pie in the sky
served with down-home hospitality
or thinly smiled hostility—depending on what you look like.

But I keep bending down those blue-dusk, distant jukebox highways
clinking long-necks with a redneck buddy of mine,
getting the funk outa there
down cracked-back back roads, tires spitting out gravel,
dust wafting up into the fine-veined, bloodshot map
of my sleep-dep, caffeine buzzed stare
that steered me all the way here, vertically speaking,
among this circle of conjurors.

If there ever was a grind it's the road
ridden the hard way—you are the car!
In this case a gut-bucket rattling, chitling jamming, no tunes,
compact, sub-standard, tin-can time machine company car
designed for going to the corner for groceries,
not for pulling show-biz Houdinis
from here to the left coast and back.

But it carried me this far to tell this raggedy tale
slammed in the door in Boston,
washed in the clarity of Walden,
Molotov cocktailed in Hell's Kitchen,
cooled in the surf of Cape Dunes,
speed-trapped in PA where it's STILL 55,
tow-jobbed in DC, caught between
an exotic dancer and the deep blue sea in FLA,
waylaid in LA by a woman with so many mouths
she'll never be satisfied, chanted into teeth
of waves in shark-bait cove on Jalama Beach,
fleeced in San Fran by my false true love,
stuck in the muck in Chaco Canyon,
crapped out luck in Vegas, and
nearly clipped off in several parts unknown—
but the shoe must go on.

Propped up by a good, bad, scalded cuppa
food-mart, non-dairy creamed 10W 40 weight joe,
I'm about a quart low, head gasket ready to blow,
in dire need of a rear-end alignment,
brake shoes shot, stuck in 5th gear for over 3 years now
and no runway ramp in sight,
mainlining that white line, high on low test,
into the small, long hours of the night,

buffeted by the wake of heavy-metal Peterbilts
wailin' *WWAAHH, WWAAHH, WWWAAAAAAAAAAHHHHH,*
leavin' me in the dark, starry outlands
where Hank's honky-tonk ghost twangs along pedal steel miles,
"Some folks say I'm no good,
that I wouldn't settle down if I could.
I love you Baby, but you gotta understand
when the Lord made me, he made a ramblin' man."

"Are you a sailor?" A salty dog asks me in Key West.
Yeah, lashed to the wheel of a '79 police blue, mule of a Ford
Fairlane or Fairmont, the cursive metal strip fell off winter's ago.
It's got a 350, 8 cylinder engine big enough
to put foil wrapped tuna-noodle casserole on the manifold
in Schenectedy and have it ready to eat by Utica,
the exhaust flavor washed down with a country cocaine cooler—
powdered aspirin and acetametaphin swirled into ice-tea.

They said I had drive—so I drove
from North Cakalaka by way of Squashed Possum
just the other side of West Hell and every fly-speck,
don't blink, twilight zone episode in between,
my home town among them, everybody locked inside,
sedated by carbohydrate comfort foods and hooked on cable.
America's happening somewhere else more real,
you just gotta channel surf to get there.
And yet here we all are, this verbal and visceral gathering.

Some days living for driving, windows wide open,
rolling alongside that gold ball settling down orange,
crosses over into the driving-for-a-living-lane,
and I'm making a living if you stretch the definition real thin.
Paycheck to paycheck. There's either a big breakthrough

around the next bend, or a nervous bustdown,
chasing that almighty buck down the pike
like it's a straggler from an ice-age herd,
trying to scrape together enough roadkill
fora cushion fora soft landing
if and when I ever do come in for one.

I've passed right on by that sign TO GET TO HEAVEN,
TURN RIGHT AND GO STRAIGHT.
I've ignored the arrow towards *BLISS*,
and one just below in the same direction towards *IGNORANCE* —
used to live down there, kind of a boring burg.
I detoured around the "Pursuit of Happiness"
suburban theme park, and lit out for the edge,
passing by signs of our times:
VOTE FOR DICK—HE'S ONE OF US.
BEER, WINE, GUNS, AMMO, PICNIC SUPPLIES.
JESUS—LORD OF OPPORTUNITY.
U.S. OUT OF NORTH AMERICA.
SEE THE WORLD'S LARGEST GROUNDHOG.
Since then I've been around the country so many times,
I ran into myself in a motel off I-40 in Tennessee,
mumbling 'where am I where am I where am I?'
Bumping into other road ghosts, my salesman father among them,
as I stumbled into a room designed the same
as every other room off every other exit
to keep one calm and sane and anonymous.
I've taken to leaving the plastic baggie on the plastic cup
to give the tap water a better taste.
I've taken to washragging the exhaust from my face
and staring into the mirror til my strung out, staggered,
3-D image gathers up into one solid shape—tired.

I've got the road map to Jersey on one side of my squint,
Oklahoma under construction on the other.
There's long stretches of Texas down my cheeks,
one too many Manhattan nights bagging my eyes,
but a Pacific coast smile under it all,
a Nawlin's wink and a big, Chicago eatin' grin.

And as I lay me down on a mattress
impressed with tons of loneliness,
decompressing from the G-force of crossing
3 times zones in one day,
that 18 wheel lullaby laps against the motel door,
and I wend my way back to that creek
sparkling under the hemlocks
down in Willoughby valley—
a simple, single green pulse
that laved away all thoughts of hurry,
all thoughts of son-of-a-salesman mortality.
But overarching it all, I-90 droned on through—four lanes,
wider than the Chagrin river, running east-west,
Boston to Chicago and beyond.
I stared at that hurry for hours from the edge of the woods,
from a hillside carved to let progress pass,
wondering where everyone was going
till one afternoon I hiked down the berm
and stuck out my thumb.

I've been riding that concrete river ever since.
Sometimes the road feels like my middle name;
I'm beginning to think it might be, by the end, my last name.
And sometimes I feel like pulling over,
picking up one of those monster truck blow-outs,
slinging it over my shoulder

and hiking far inland on trails the Shawnee walked and talked
where only deer browse now,
until some forgotten hillbilly kin asks me,
"What the hell are you doing with that thing?
Sit down, I'll tell you a story"—
those wheels within wheels carried me here,
between the rushes of business, *WWAAAHHH, WWWAAAHHH,*
WWWWWWWAAAAAAAAAAAAAAAAHHHHHHHHH,
over miles and miles of orange barrels and tired smiles
in middle of the night doorways at the end of the line...
among this circle of conjurors,
where all the poetry starts.

Homage to the Monotony of Summer

Under unfurled pools of green sun,
catkins hang,
effusing pungencies that conjure up
a swirling eddy of bugs glinting
through shafts of sunlight.
One coppery-bodied, orange-eyed, iridescent-winged fly
bends a fescue stem
in front of where I sit crosslegged
in a park surrounded by the hub-bub of Boston.

And in that span of delicate silence,
the homely, rolling, July hills around Barlow, Ohio
unfold again—rows of corn on and on,
and pastures of cows, the acrid weight of Holstein stink
wafted on the gift of a breeze,
their lowing flowing over a rise,
or a single moo elongating through a cool hollow.
Aways up alternate route 550, the horizon
wavers over the tar, that blur
where day meets dream,
where I first sensed distances opening
inside as far as outside
and bee-lined the yellow flaring corn
to an oak smack dab in the middle of the field—
left there for shade, for lightening, for the fact it stood
too mighty hoary to bring down.
And I climb up again for a long look
at tired, green dog hills hunkering down
as time hums all around
and not at all,
calming me to the dumb stare of a cow—

Wherein the measures of the monotony
overlap...the tomatoes on the sill
turning from yellow-orange to swollen red to soft black...
Grandma counting cars from the window, figuring
how many pass by in a given hour, memorizing
The Book of Ruth between...
The thump and swish of quarter horses in the next field
already plodding towards pools of shade
through silvered weeds that burn off golden by noon...
The one-hundred and seventy-five pound flathead catfish
on a stringer in Veto Lake,
its vivid gills strumming muddy bottom...
The hell of the long heat spells, dry spells, plain old spells
of summer punctuated
by a horsefly bite, a thunderstorm, or Grandma
calling again through the afternoon I circled
and circled, my buzzing engulfed
in a flourish of green stillness.

How Spring Came and Went Down Centre Street

Twice before among the sullen faces
on the bus in this so far dingy Spring,
I caught your face open, lambent and hinting.
Then once more last week I was lucky,
you walking towards me, everything
on the street happening as if underwater.
This third time's a charm, a chance, I stood
jammed with impatience and possibilities.

You gave not a wink but a quirky upturn
of your mouth, a quick scan of my manhood
and breezed past. That look from the depths
of your umber eyes left me there beautifully
stupified, grounding me in this body,
and sending a panache up from my roots.

Cocky then, I watched until you were just
about to sashay around the corner.
And knowing my following your long black hair
anywhere all along, you turned and tossed back
a touche—there between your teeth was the red
sprig plucked from me as you passed by.

Staggered again, I stepped out of my body
and back in—the street washed clean
as after a cloud-burst. The tacky neon signs
PIZZA, LIQUOR, and BUDGET MEN'S WEAR
glowed like dogwoods, magnolias and azaleas.
Hundreds of windows shut tight since fall
were thrown open to the day suddenly May.

I somnambulated into a coffee shop to gather
my wits, but couldn't stop glancing out.
Rationale clicked in then, dressed in his neat
insurance salesman's suit and smirked,
"Come on, how long do flowers last anyway?"
I looked away, sipping my coffee sweet and creamy,
tasted as if for the first, the last time.

Boston Salsa

Dominicanos on the corner
in Boston in late March,
hands shoved into thin
pockets, shift from foot
to foot in alligator shoes,
cursing the lingering winter
air into flamboyant plumes
in front of island faces.

Soon salsa will bloom and
boom hot through the hood,
vibrating window panes,
the sun a trumpet
blaring every morning
as customized rides
meringue into evening,
timbales bubbling up
through the tropical
triple-decker nights.

But now it is still
winter on the corner
in Boston where they shift
from foot to foot, breaths
freezing into flamboyant
"Que cojones frio" plumes
in front of island faces.

At the Statue of Mary Dyer

[HANGED IN BOSTON, 1660]

Mary Dyer, head and eyes downcast
but calm, bonnet and bodice proper,
hands folded doves in her lap,
sits in defiant conscience and waits
to be hanged on the Common
for saying her inner light out loud.

What possessed her was worse,
in the mind of the community,
than smallpox, typhus, or syphilis.
On a day as plain as grey homespun,
forced to confess, she would not
relent her spirit, and so was cast out
by the Elders and left to swing—
a reminder of the presence of Evil,
how He takes a woman, fills her
with molten lead, leads her astray
into their midst, and abandons her.

On the scaffold, she must have known
there was no pit of hell below,
nor a righteous Father above—
that up was the same as down
when light filled all.
But how solemn could she have remained
when her six-stone weight dropped,
snapped the light out of her eyes
and flung it on their faces—
faces worn stolid from their doubt
of being one of the elect?

The blue saliva of strangulation,
the sudden mess of her organs
jarred to letting go—
they had a body on their hands
then, the corrupt flesh.
There, the abstraction, "heretic,"
went slack, the threat reduced
to "the baseness of woe-to-man."
She swung there until the day
faded, and propriety called,
after the Common stood empty
except for the beasts of the field,
for her removal and burial
under the embers of sunset.

Washing the Window

One would think whatever makes one
even speculate on the molten eons
that fused the granite boulder over there,
the upheavals that percolated it apart,
the ice-age that pushed it along,
the next ice-age that scored and deposited it
behind these row-houses standing here
in the middle of the city a mere hundred years,
one would think that leap of faith to the rock of ages
would suffice for miraculous —

that whatever urge makes one spelunk
the animal, vegetable, mineral cranium
down the brain-stem to the core single cell
semi-permeable squib of dreaming plasm which once
upon forever squirmed from ocean drop and climbed
out on the limb of breathing, hunger, desire and vision,
confirms that what one calls oneself
has been present some way, shape or form continuously,
the great ceremony of being wholly.

Those mastodons grazing the back lawn,
and those cardboard, color picture mastodons
on pages turned by pudgy fingered opposable thumb,
and those dead bits of fire, and ocher mastodons
flickering on the cave-wall TV screen
all hover conjured by that same aforementioned quirk
glinting along the optic nerve.

But the phone ringing brings one
back to the chore at hand, washing the windows

so the fall leaves seem to burn more clearly,
but the phone ringing brings one
to notice the wrought-iron bars on the window coming loose
and the holiday break-in season is just around the corner,
but the phone ringing brings one
to pick it up and say nothing.
And someone asks a name, taking life through
years of a story together. One hangs up then
and looks through the just-washed window
at that granite boulder, the sun burning, the earth
turning, and another ice-age creeping down.

Objective Postcard

The sky dead
pigeon grey
clumped against
library granite.

Waiting for you
in the courtyard
the fountain withered
and blew away years ago.

Old news sits stacked
on a chair, the words
string along dull
as a line of ants.

No place to go
today where I would be
less objective than
the last time we held,

you asleep in my arms,
breathing, a naked fact.

Postcard from a Window in the Orange Line El

Boston cold, grey evening
rush-hour on the Orange Line El.
Mirror skyscrapers scream power
at each other. Everybody's spent—
especially whoever stepped under
the subway's grind gumming up
the commute for the rest of us.
The inbound screeches past
like a sick and tired ejaculation
of an old man in a coldwater
Single Room Occupancy Hotel
along the tracks. Down below,
a fishnetted girl in a leather mini
dances a shiver on the corner.
Up the street in Colonial tombs, vets
stay warm till the cops clean them out.
Another inbound train scours past.
The girders sag and rain flakes of rust
settling over small patches of moss.

The Day Ed Donnegan Died

> "Where are the lads I loved so well
> all back on the Shamrock shore?"

The day Ed Donnegan came to Amerikay
together with his cousin from Mayo,
"right then and there on the Boston Quay,"
they argued over where the hell they were to go
and parted ways for good from the only family
either knew in these western counties.

The day Ed Donnegan went back down to the docks
was the first of weeks on end as a stevedore,
"haulin' sacks, packin' crates and shots knocked back."
"I said, haulin' sacks, packin' crates and shots knocked back,"
at the end of the day for well on forty years
of keeping his big brogued foot in the door.

That day, fifty years later, Donnegan the lame
crashed down the rooming house stairwell
all the way to the empty bottle bottom,
his crutches were his only relations, skeletal.
No more a roving the rolling hills of Mayo
me boyo, o no, o no, me boyo, no.

The day Ed Donnegan laid there spilled out
at the bottom of the stairs the better part of a day,
the other roomers, "all drunken louts,"
took bids on helping him up anyway.
"I'll do it for twenty. A ten. A fiver,
but listen, Donnegan, that's our final offer"

The day Ed Donnegan died, no-one came to pray
his soul to keep, no women came to keen,
let alone to haul his body away
from Amerikay across the silver shining ocean
back to Mayo, o no, o no, me boyo,
will you be roving the rolling hills of Mayo.

Elegy for Joe Bent

Joe, I did not know you well
alive. I meant to visit again
to listen to fish stories.
I meet you now, sunken
in a casket, your face made
over, but even so, sagging.
Sometimes I'm just too tired
to mourn, so many have gone by.
Today there is no movement
inside but anger that you were
John Doe to most, unnoticed,
your seventy years brought down
to one room and a box of clothes.

Even as I mention this, somebody
lets do their final inhale.
The heart, chest and throat muscles
relax in a release never felt
before, the bliss of giving up
before one passes on. I hope
it was that easy for you
the morning of your last walk,
easy as the prow of a trawler
splitting the calm inside the Cape.
Joe, I never did get back to you,
and so many have gone by now.

There, the Charles River in late fall.
There, that good pull I feel then.
Then you will come to me and go,

when the banks have gone brown,
when the water runs high and dark,
full of small, random whirlpools,
I will see you doddering along
the street again, in baggy pants,
your shirt open and blowing,
simply amused by your motion.

At Seaside Nursing Home

They sit gossiping in the lobby
of the home where everyday they sink
a little more into their memories.

She dozes, bored of the droning, though
she keeps herself on the edge
of the conversation by nodding now

and again when they ask, did you hear
who died last week? She yawns and yearns
to be free of tea and elegies.

At night she watches the flash of waves,
slides asleep under that wide water
and dreams of thousands of darting silvers.

Far out in the calm, in the undisturbable
depths, silicon caskets of crustaceans
and bleached wafers of plankton settle

like a snowfall across the rifts,
in the crevices, and down the meadows
where she feels the drift of light.

Postcard, New York City

The beautiful New
Yorkers can buy the sun
and wear it toned
and ready for fashions
all through the grey
faces of winter streets.
Their eyes shine
like island vacations,
hearts as colorful
as magazines fanned.
They rise and reflect
in tall glass boxes.
They dine and excrete
millions. They move
down Madison Avenue
as if they are being
filmed, as if they are
as powerful as money.

Hit and Run

I just came out of the subway yesterday,
I was going to do some shopping after work,
right there by that boutique on the corner,
and there's this bag, a used, brown-paper bag
torn open in the middle of the street with a loaf
of bread, some old bananas and a grapefruit squished
like it was run over, I mean Boston drivers are so crazy,
and there was a crowd of people like me on the curb,
and O my god there was this old man laying face down in the
    street,
and there was no-one near him—it must have been a hit
and run that just happened—no-one standing there did it,
and there was no car stopped, and time was moving in slow-motion.
The guy was old. Homeless maybe. Well, kind of poor looking.
I could see his big shabby coat and baggy pants from the curb,
and it was so nice out yesterday. I didn't want to get any closer
because of the AIDS and all even though there wasn't any blood,
but there was this clear fluid coming out of his ear, really gross,
and there was this woman wailing to high heaven in some language,
Portuguese maybe, like he was her baby or something, but
    obviously
she didn't even know him, I mean he was this old, white guy,
    a bum,
I mean nobody seemed to know him, and this stretch limo was
    stuck
in traffic and this woman, she looked kind of famous, stuck her
    head
out the window and then ducked back in and the window slid
    back up
and I left. I went into this store that was right there, I mean
I don't even know what it was, it was just to get off the street,

and the girl behind the counter smiled and asked if she could
    help me,
and some guy comes in the store right behind me and just stands
    there
really quiet and I thought he was going to say something to me or
    something.
I mean he just stood there forever, and then he says, "he's dead."
Like he was talking to me and I don't know him from Adam, and
    I looked
at the girl behind the counter and she looks back at me, and he
    left.
But I couldn't shop anymore, I mean, I knew what I wanted—
    some wine
glasses and black & white place settings—but I couldn't shop I
just kept seeing that dirty old paper bag and that squished
    grapefruit,
but I'm glad she was crying like that even though it bothered me
    at first.

The Savior of Times Square

Babylon's walls stare a million blank eyes
over a million passersby focused on success
as I stumble prayer of feet through Grand Central Chaos
towards sign of the Times Squared at pitch of dis,
the writing on the wall flashing past with a hiss.

"Jesus is knocking on the door of your heart today!"
someone intones along the traffic-jammed street.
Black Sunday fedora, black topcoat to his feet,
he bows and bellows, echoing off scuffled concrete,
"Jesus is knocking on the door your heart today."

Who is this black bell rasping proclamation,
the crow perched on the shoulder of the cross,
croaking a dirge before stropping beak on skin?
Or is this Saint Judas come back to tell us,
"Don't you know who that is you just let pass?"

"Jesus is knocking on the door of your heart today,"
rolling away tombstones from eyes to vision
of strangers' flesh as it catches fire and shines
from child's face of innocence and grace,
shadows falling to reveal none other than

Jesus Baglady mumbling psalms around waste-basket;
Jesus Businessman rendering unto, checking his shackle;
Jesus Mohammed Cabby honking warning at Jesus Angel fishnets;
MCJC, gold-chained glowering revolution under bandana;
Jesus Mary Joseph Beat cop pinching donut in fist.

"Hey, whaddya lookin' at? Move it along!"
Jesus is knocking on the badges of the philistines;
on the screens of brokers bilking another million;
on peepshow plexiglass, junky veins, chamber of gun,
empty, as neighbors meet their maker, trespasses forgiven.

So Judas kissed Jesus and Jesus returns the kiss
on the other cheek, "Give this to the next you meet."
And Judas, helping the thieves down from their crosses,
kisses them awake from nails to indivisible light,
"Jesus is knocking on the door of your heart today..."

Leaving me standing before a wall of ID cards,
yellowing faces behind glass of name-change store.
And in the middle of those reborn cons and aliens
hangs an 8 x11 crown of thorns 3-D head-shot of Christ—
tilt this way his agony, tilt that way he expires,

so your own face reflects superimposed over his.
'How much for the Saviour?' I ask the proprietor,
leaning in the doorjamb, surveying the tide of customers.
All he says is like he says it all day is, "$19.99"—
sale of century, over population, millenium count down.

Ah, Jesus, keep your damn religion off his back.
Not Jesus End-times or Jesus Money, just peace.
Let him pass through this world in Judas' wake,
whispering in your ear the kiss of your own pulse,
Jesus is knocking on the door of your heart today.

High Time

"A classic week-end blow-out,"
you call it through razor-scraped voice.
"Tootin night into day into night into
blowin off Monday morning work to boot,"
lickin the last of the talcum-cut traces
from the slit of a cracked mirror. Your skull
surfaces through a year's worth of grind
and binge, denial and lies smilin up
with a plastic straw up your nose as
you talk shit about that shit, how it's
just continuing research on addiction.
Try gettin straight you wanna really
explore it, crawlin the walls scrawlin out
the twisted trail of all you're tryin to kill
till you fall shriveled and wasted
on the blank sheets of your notebook.
You went and did it alright,
snorted the last few cents left
for one more buzzin run ...from
or towards? You don't even know anymore.
But runnin away, runnin away has a way
of catchin up with you—the second wind
turns into the third, gaspin. It's fourth
down inches to go and the final seconds
tic, tic, tic through your wired brain—
snap, synapse collapse as you leap
over the goal line last stand.
But it's never the free falling,
it's that sudden stop. Short.
And everybody's gone, the drunken fans,
the cheerleaders, especially her,

and your empty as that bitter
plastic baggy rollin across the field.

Now you sit the game on the sidelines.
Grey fills everyday, a stringy drizzle
fizzlin out as cars swish by
in their usual hurry. It comes down
to a shrunken room, your world tilted
towards that dull hell that defines alone,
"any lower and I'd be six feet under."
It's finally high time to arm-wrestled him.
Knock that candy outa his bony hand,
look him straight in his glazed eyes
forgive him, but pin him down for good.

Down Mount Greylock on a Winter Evening

Talking along, one of us notices
the mesh of birch on the mountainside,
breath hovering over snowfields.
None of us have ever spoken a word.

Hitchhiking

The Cyclops sun stares, sears
afternoon hours
from center of sky.
Stuck on a wavering
stretch of tar, I'm hot
as a grasshopper's brain
on the end of a stalk
and still waiting
for a ride. The withering breath
of what's left of a breeze
strokes hollow yellow weeds,
stokes cicadas to a dull churn
and stops inches
before my face.

Dust devils gust up
and die out around a raggy,
splintered road-kill staring
flat up from berm
wild eyes frozen
with speed of light—
never made it to cover,
to be taken under
out of the way
of what's called 'progress'.
Man, I see whole peoples run over
down this road paved with the need
to flee whatever fell apart
back in Eden.

Left off outside Coolville, Ohio,
bump in the road
where my old man was born
in a boarding house boarded up
by now, or a fast food lot,
God knows.
Ain't never been there
and I'm passing by again—

Passing by same as that parched horsefly
dragging a long drone in its wake
forlorn as a bluegrass high lonesome
about the sweet by and by ...
only I'm still standing here
waiting for another good ol' boy,
fire and brimstone fearin' Samaritan
to pull over in an air-conditioned
American Dream and save
more than my soul:

"You have a girlfriend, Son?
now I know what you're thinking,
but I ain't one of them.
it's just that you look like
a fine, healthy young man to me,
and I'd hate to see you burn
down below for some terrible sin.
I don't mean back behind the barn
necking with snooty little Mary Lou.
I mean that down and dirty stuff.
What do you call it, 'bumpin' uglies?'
You ever done any of that, Son?

No, now it's none of my business,
but Jesus is my business, yes, Sir.
And we are all on a mission to save
one and other. It's the Lord's Plan
to hasten the rapture. The Rapture!
when the Second Coming comes, Son.
The way I was taught you has to admit
you're a sinner before you earn grace.

Now I'll tell you exactly what I do
every time I get the urge to 'bump uglies.'
I make my wife kneel right down
beside the bed. Then I kneel down.
And you know what we do then?
We ask God to forgive us both
for all the dirt we're about to do.
That's what you ought to do, Son.
Ask God to forgive you for getting
all dirtied up with a woman.
if you'd like we can stop at my house
and pray it all out together."

No Sir, I'm not looking for no
promised land, just a lift down the road.
I stand and squint
and know I can go anywhere
I want and I'll return
to the sedges crowding
around that culvert yonder,
burgeoning what damp
lingers during this drought,
a column of gnats
glinting, sticking mud.

I reach down, pinch a stem
and the tincture medicines
my senses awake
to my father who art not
in heaven but rooted hereabouts,
this flickering life
green flames confirm.

Postcard from Chick's Lounge

The Kanawa Valley haze
downwind from Dow Chemical
eats away at CHICK'S LOUNGE,
handpainted sign over a shack
between the strip club
and the hubcap resale shop
on pot-holed Ohio river road.
"Chick," name of dad's buddy,
maybe the bar where he ended up
had he lived. But his liver gave out,
some long time gone now.
Dad and him, "Bud" and "Chick,"
drove a milktruck through hollers
and hills outside Marietta
all through high school
every day well before sun-up.
The pure, cold clink and rattle
of white and empty bottles in racks
bouncing over dirt roads
made music to their ears
as they back and forthed motorcycles
and leather flight jackets,
and how they were going
to get out of that backwater
in the days before rock and roll.
One morning one fall years later,
Chick nearly froze to death
on our back stoop in the suburbs
outside Cleveland's steel mills
far from those hills.
Too ashamed to knock, he waited

till Dad got up for work to take him in.
He sat shaking at the kitchen table.
Dad handed him a cup of joe,
poured the milk for him, clattering.
He was still twitching
through a broken smile
when I came home from school.
And ramshackle CHICK'S LOUNGE
is locked up like nobody has been
blind drunk in there in a while.
I drive on, cinders crunching
and spitting softly from my tires.
The ghosts of these hills are thirsty
for a drink of clear water.

Postcard, Ohio Valley Pear

Southern Ohio Appalachian fall unfolds,
the whole Hocking valley ripe
and repeating its colors on up near foothills,
flourished, then over a far slope.

The ground that has been holding its breath exhumes
into the smoulder of things,
and a beagle yelps off on the scent down the blue light
of a hollow, its howl falling
off but faintly lingering as I pause to eat
this leftover Bartlett pear full
and seeping the valley's yellow glow.

If I do end up in some black and white movie of a city,
it will come down to this pear—
without its flavor I could never make it back to carry
over, each of these hills, yes, here.

The Discovery of Pluto

The night of February the nineteenth,
their Lord nineteen-hundred and thirty,
winter rattled the blackened oaks
in Coolville, Athens County, Ohio.
My father had been alive around
five months. His heart was soft,
strong, no bigger than his fist.
But he never had much luck from the start.
He came into this world three weeks
before the stock market crashed.

On the coldest night in their living
memory, Pluto, ninth planet in this system,
was in fact seen for the first time.
It's orbit had been predicted
from Neptune's, which had, in its turn,
been placed from the eccentric warp
of Uranus. Not one observer had noted,
or could note for that matter, curved space
and contracting time
wearing it down to crystals.

Three-hundred thousand or so books
would have to be altered in their details.
What could my father, a newborn, do then
and there about all that science but cry.
So, like the mouth he was, he did—
hungry, new planet or not.

No-one heard him but his mother
and his father, dying already and forever

dreaming of better times—and me, now.
Everybody else had their own
problems getting by on the edge
of Appalachia at the beginnings
of the depression. They had no idea
it was out there, a new world,
let alone how far away it spun.

But Clyde W. Tombaugh, obscure astronomer,
stood proud under the desert stars that night,
wholly occupied with that speck
of ice—and good for him.

So now what logical turns of matter
whirling away outside and inside somebody
wait for figures and words that the slightest
child's cry will crack into meaning?

Skill

The filament glistened across the first light,
the line carried by the sinker arcing and falling
right where it was aimed
without startling the surface.
Reeling in, and again the zip of the release, whizz of the spool
and slip of the jig.
Skill, my old man found around the stumps and tangles,
dropping a lure where the crappies hover unhurried.
Zip, whizz, slip—easy as pie, flashing his salesman's smile.
Not so much to catch anything but to cast,
the accomplishment of hitting the right spot after three or four
    tries,
brought on that smile. The repetitions,
the light weight of the line thrown all morning, evened out the
    pressure.
The next season, before we returned to the dawn water,
before he made it to his two weeks, he'd be broke and dead
a fourth and final time when a clot stopped the flow.

To prepare for that vacation, I scrawled a long plea
for the supplies arrayed on the back page of a comic book
that I creased and placed on his pillow.
Three rods, a box full of lures and a floating knife—
all for only $19.99 what a deal!
In my room I waited for him to fight through rush-hour,
listened for him creaking up the stairs, his briefcase
heavier than my tackle-box.
He closed the door and it stayed closed.
Later, my mother told me we couldn't afford it right now.

Selling would never be fishing.
Oh, they got away more often than not, the big ones.

You didn't get paid for a beautiful cast or for patience,
but for a client.
It became less and less easy for him to rise every seven o'clock,
steam of coffee from his thermos mingling not with the mist
off the lakes and creeks back home,
but with the exhausted fumes of Carnegie Avenue.

Zip, whizz, slip, the meditation he could not find time for.
Day in, day out, too much the perfectionist, he would make
    his pitch,
his handshakes strained, the face beneath his face fatigued,
his smile sagging a little more with each effort—
the line caught on another snag, jerked, and snapped.

The Snapping Turtle Holding On

I've seen full grown ones
first hand, one when my uncle
and me went frog-gigging
in Butcher Holler near Barlow.
He nearly broke his wooden leg
in a sink-hole that night—
tough folks, Appalachians.
He speared a good dozen
I froze in a flashlight beam,
enough for our breakfast.
At dawn he hefted up a trot-line
with a creature from eons ago
on the other end. Jaws and claws
thrashed from under black-ridged,
algae-tufted shell one-third my size—
a female, we found out later
when he turned it on its back
and split it open, eggs spilling
bright orange across the grass.
He cut and put chunks of her
into the freezer, along with
a surplus of chicken pot-pies
bought at the Marietta supermarket.
They'd eat every last bite.
They know how to get by
in those hills. They had to.

The creeks up North where we moved
were turned into open sewers.
Even so, we caught one once
trundling overland towards
the rusty blue-sludge effluent

near a row of new machine-shops.
I stepped in front of it
in my rubber boots. Hissing,
it sunk its beak into the toe
of my boot and would not let go.
They've been known to hold on
even after the head is severed off.
Reggie pried it loose with a stick
and it plowed through the weeds,
smelling for water, sliding
down the culvert and burrowing
under the sludge. Who knows
how long it stayed down there
before poking up its snout.
Men have dated fossils of them
three hundred million years old.
I still go back to look for it.
Too many other machine shops
to count have opened along the creek
since then, giving work to men
with house payments and mouths
to feed, men who have a dim
yearning to be green again,
who manage to get to the woods once
or twice a year, get drunk
and shoot anything that moves.

Intricate

Intricate
rosette
mandala,
one cell
plankton
in the face
of starry
turnings,
phosphorescent
glimmer of
nativities,
only sheer membrane
contains
dream
osmosing,
synapses
light years
apart
arc a
circuit—
then through
this thick
glow of krill
a blue
whale
roils up,
strains tons
of ocean,
swallowing
all
throught

The Whistle and Nothing

God but I wanted to dance with the dead.
St. Patrick's night, embalmed with beer,
my body numb and dumb, thick as stout,
I stumbled home by way of the graves.

I jarred my head open like a crypt,
waiting, ready for the white rustling
of wraiths' gowns over flat, worn stones,
for flecks of moon jiggling with shadows.

My pasty lips creaked out a fetching tune,
a whistle that quivered like the plucked guts
of a fiddle, then seethed down to nothing
through clumsy markers and pithy oaks.

My Old Man

H-A-Double R-I-G-A-N spells Harrigan,
Proud of all the Irish blood that's in me,
Devil the man to say a word again' me.
H-A-Double R-I-G-A-N you see,
That's the man with the name
Shame can never be connected with,
Harrigan, that's me!

My old man never made it to be an old man, a drummer
beating his feet, knocking on one more door of opportunity
opening away from Appalachian Depression boyhood,
success just a Horatio Alger get-rich-quick handshake away
as he climbed from stock-clerk to sales-rep to desk job,
selling those dental equipment smiles and finding his ladder up
against the wrong building when he finally made it to the top —
not a Broadway marquee. A would-be Vaudeville hoofer,
he'd croon corny, Irish-American moldy-oldies on the drive
back from the office, by-passing high blood pressure
Cleveland rush-hour by way of Pat Joyce's piano bar —
still carrying those tunes up the back stairs
of that last place we never rented long enough to call home,
tapping wingtip brogues through routines scuffled across
cracked kitchen linoleum floors with a kick-ball-change,
kick-ball-change in a wake of whiskey, nicotine punch lines
curling back on his smile under bare-bulb stage light
with a bah-rump-dah wink he tossed to me hiding in the corner.

Always after road trips I'd hear him straining up those stairs
like there were bricks in his briefcase, like it was full
of 65 dead gold-plated wristwatches, packed tight
with the ashes of every pack of cigs smoked to kill time,

heavy with the wet sand from the creek down home,
the creek he never made it back to, the creek trickling out
of a holler past a billboard of a lone ship on a vast sea
JOIN THE NAVY, SEE THE WORLD. He did, to Korean War,
drinking a round with USO show touring Donald O' Conner
and picking up a few steps to boot, with a kick-ball-change, light
as the flicker of Cagney as George M. Yankee-doodle-dandyin'
White house steps on the screen of the Marietta Picture show.
But the stairs and his joints creaked with the weight
of what must have sounded, by the end, like failure. A silence
sunk in his eyes I could not guess then, that early-grave
stare I've seen since, that salesman during happy-hour,
gazing off into the mirror for wherever his life went.
I took him, for an instant, for my father.

His charm and blarney and Kennedy blue-serge suits
danced against failed deals and calls from bill collectors.
No matter how much he believed that smile could sell — it wilted
as useless as the at-peace pasty one pulled across his face
for his forty-year old, lace-casket lined curtain call.
I'm looking over a four-leafed clover
that I've over-looked before.
One leaf is sunshine, the second is rain,
third are the roses that grow in the lane
I'm looking over his smiling, Irish eyes now, closed —
not my father, but a brother, worn out by one too many
wrong turns turning out to be dead ends.
How he must have sang open his new offices
and closed them down with a shuffling exit stage left.

Always I heard him straining up those winding stairs
a god-damned tired ghost of the Depression

following one step behind, his own old man
hunching home from the mines in rags.
He'd close that bedroom door and it stayed closed.
But sometimes still I'm wakened to a summer morning
born for fishing, the first light slanting through
the back porch screen, wakened by someone
watching over me. And I look up at him smiling down,
"Buddy, let's get this show on the road," kick-ball-change...

Ice Floes on the Hock-Hocking Near Athens, Ohio

Once upon a time there was
Irish ways and Irish laws.
We are a river flowing.
We are a river flowing.

Stout on top of stout down at O'Hooley's,
we were cracking into a regular ceiliedh

when Jimmy Prouty calls TIME! And kicks us out
into a winter cold snap where we all stood about

chattering, the fiddle, mandolin and pipes
stopped and too cold to put bottle to lips.

So all music and most dowdling over,
I made my way down to the breaking river

with an inkling of a tinkling of an I day
to sing this chronic, Celtic melancholy away.

What did I learn from my culture but to drink
and slur nostalgic songs sooner than think.

Not another noise on the Hock-Hocking but ice
fissures hissing or a piece jarring loose,

a ghost bobbing the flow, gnashing its teeth
against bridge pilings. I'm wishing my own breath

recalled one or two good, Gaelic expletives
to hurl at the current. I'm ready to give

hell to passers-by in the name of Ireland
just for the sound of it, ouskey-ban pride,

but the only Irish I have left is my name—
as passing as this Shawnee, as passing as the Shannon.

> *Once upon a time there was*
> *Irish ways and Irish laws.*
> *We are a river flowing.*
> *We are a river flowing.*

Remembering Ulster

I'm remembering a dismembered Ulster—
the red hand hacked from the sailor's own arm
and thrown ashore to lay claim on the land;
the severed head of Blessed Oliver Plunkett,
a shrunken leathery stare housing mites now,
surveying the remains of martyrdom
from the sunken hulk of a medieval cathedral;
the rebels who Cromwell drew and quartered
and impaled on the walls of (London) Derry
in the name of the one, true God;
the Planters grafting themselves anew
on trees nurtured under centuries before;
the murals of arms on grey project walls,
arms rising from flames, breaking chains,
brandishing guns; the scattered clans,
violated treaties, Celtic bodies of Brits,
Welsh, Scots and Irish blasted by plastics.

When I finally went back to my roots I found them
tangled, sucking the blood-brother's feud
from the oul' sod, the soil rising
twisted as a blackthorn from the Glens of Antrim—
tattooing the sky with its gory story,
beating the lambegh, beating the bodhran
till the hands bleed again. I was trying
to piece together the place I came from,
gawking at locals like they were living fossils,
seeing a face shaped like my sister Pat's,
the Viking stature of my sister Micki,
the green eyes, dark hair and olive skin of Maureen,
my own close set eyes staring back
from the carved stele of Clonmacnoise

"A very old, Gaelic name," the professor claimed,
"stretching back to Conchubar MacNessa,
King of Ulster. And Traitor." The lineage
cut to "Mick" by the English, mutilated
further by Protestants to M apostrophe
to exorsize the ghost of their own ancient tongue.

"M'Niece," the stern old Orangeman, the last
of his line, pronounced it in Larne townland
where my name fell on both sides of the divide.
"There's another with the name down the lane,
but you don't want to have anything to do with them."
Just the same could you tell me where they live?
"It's easy," he said, eyeing me now with contempt
reserved for those lazy, dirty, lying others,
"they're the only ones without the red, white and blue
painted-on their curb." "Catholics," the boy confirmed,
"For as long as any of me Uncles can remember."
And as he walked me to the door and no further,
he called after me in the gathering dark,
"We have a saying here in the North, the English
can't remember the past and the Irish can't forget."
I make my way back to back to America, looking
over my shoulder for shadows, for bloody footprints.

Vedron Smelovic Plays an Adagio for Sarajevo (Thomasini Albioni)

Under the dull whump and
whump and whump of the morning's
round of mortars
stomping the foot of god-hate through Sarajevo;
below the damp pop,
pop-pop-pop, pop of snipers
cleansing another neighborhood
like boys potting rats off a dump;
beneath the wait
of the next note to crescendo
muffled wreckage,
Vedron Smelovic wakes—

wakes as he has done
for the last 21 days on end,
takes his concert tuxedo
from where it hangs close by,
pulls it on upright,
straightens his black tie
and walks out without flinching
towards the bakery
where 22 people in line that morning
never heard what blew them to bits.
He carries the hollow
body of the cello close
through streets of burnt-out storefronts
glaring across at each other
and stops at a particular crator.
Setting up a folding stool, he leans

the neck against his shoulder and pauses
to wipe the fine flour of ash
from the polished wood lightly—

lightly as a mother brushing a crumb
of sweetbread from the down
above her crying child's lip,
lightly as the young lovers just ahead in line
smile the future reflecting
in each other's face,
lightly as the man just behind laughs,
a little embarrassed by their predicament,
but holding his place in line
just the same—

and lightly Vedron Smelovic's calloused fingers
slide into the first few notes,
pulling and pushing and pulling the last
of the 22 lives in line
free from the debris of statistics.
From the empty body,
from the blackened eyes,
from the weary strings,
this mourning flows, overflows.
When will humanity see
we are one family,
from the same tree,
one family?

Great Grandma Kocejve of Llubljana

At night the unlocked double-doors float open
and she glides down sanitarium hallways,
hands held before her, fingers rippling
like water poured into a porcelain basin.
Her backless gown flutters glowing
as footfalls descend fragile arpeggios
of a nocturne played on a glass harpsichord.

She's been told repeatedly to keep her hands
busy—she rubs fingertips pinpricked
by years of stitching, cooling their crookedness
on the bones of keys stroked like holy relics.
The notes pattern silence into a golden cage
from which she flies every morning, f-tha, f-tha,
f-tha splayed against the dirty windowpanes
where orderlies find her, the sun pouring through
rusty bars, her hands still sending this music.

A Mongrel on the Edge of the Flats

(for the Annual Labor Day Junk-Stock Reading)

From the middle of this rusting junkyard
at the edge of the chain-linked-fenced Flats,
it does not look like the end of the world today
to this dog. His forebears chased gas-guzzling hulks
that once drove long and shiny out of nearby plants.
They sink into oil-pits now, gulls stuck on their backs
There's nothing left to guard here 'cause you can't fit
an 8 cylinder, 350 Cleveland engine on a computer chip.

Fried-food smells and over-priced drink laughter
waft up from the new clubs along the Cuyahoga
that burned off its stinking skin three decades ago.
Bored Dog chases his raggedy tail, bedding down
tall grass no longer there—force of habit.
Summer rots fragrantly away somewhere Southeast.
He sniffs a shred of it on the breeze
threading across exhausted freeways.

He dozes and twitches, dreaming of running
through fields of plump, stumbling rabbits.
He nightmares Dick and Jane prancing
over a green sward along a picket fence
with him as a clean Spaniel trotting behind
smiling—startled awake, he looks around
and wonders why dogs ever began hanging
with two-leggers in the first place.

They seemed to be heading to the top
of the food chain at the time. They had those

pointy sticks and fire to cook the fat.
Couches couldn't be too far down the line.
He barks at nothing but steel Cleveland sagging,
rising as glass boxes in magnificent ignorance.
The sun sets over the Flats warming this rug.
He yawns, his pink tongue curling and uncurling.

The Definition of Making a Living

(for the Bernie Firestone Labor Conference)

...work, beer, food, tv, sex, sleep...work
beer, food, tv, sleep...work, beer, food, sleep...
work, beer, sleep...work, sleep...worse
than 9 to 5, or 7 to 3, or 3 to 11, it's 11 to 7 plus
mandatory overtime "ya don't like it, take a hike."
And you've taken on the shape of lifting the bulk
of the Industrial Revolution for the last 200 years,
bent spine, stooped shoulders, tough, stringy biceps
and punched-in gut swelling up with cheap beer.
You've gone form a 6-pack, to a 12-pack, to the suitcase—
living the hi-life in the land of tool and dying.

And guts is not telling how you can't take it no more
when the kid is screaming in the middle of the night
like he's never gonna stop, like nothing you could do
could ever make life happy, and the mantra that keeps
ringing through your ears, the bones hammered dull
as hell, the mantra that keeps you going when you
throw your feet outa bed in the morning, and your boots
moan, "no, no," is your wallet whining, "you gotta, man."
There's still no Labor Page, but the Business Section says
"downsize" so often it makes you wince with years of no
fight, no flight even though they never laid a hand on ya.

So you go in and punch the clock and punch the clock and
punch the clock and punch and punch the clock just to lift
that rusting hulk of progress and push it down the road
one more mile, clinging to its side, monkey-wrenching
the last lug-nut on the engine block as it spits

burnt-out oil in your lungs and belches blue death
through your brain so you can't think anymore.
It's no longer a matter of harnessing power or
control—you're just trying to steer it now
to a soft landing somewhere over that next hill
of promised land, somewhere like the suburbs.

Foreman give the downwardly-mobile sons of the broken
dream the once over when they apply at the shops,
They know they won't last more than a paycheck or two
next to 150 degree molds and earsplitting deburring.
They'd rather be screaming heavy-metal into mics
til their heads explode than humping the grind.
But they'll be back after they blow their last two bucks
on a WIN FOR LIFE scratch ticket cause you gotta
match three to win. They'll be back when their backs
are still strong, their eyes burning and their hands ready
to freeze into the shape of holding onto the machine.

Houseflies 1955

She sips her coffee, zips
the best brew, 'a perky pick-me-up.'
On TV it stutters ecstatically
into the plastic bulb on top of the pot.
But the grounds in the sink stick as black
as his stubble in the bathroom sink,
as the seconds' tick marks on all the clocks,
as the dots that make up the picture screen,
as the pupils of her eyes shrunken.

She has done the dishes, sanitized
the bathroom, sprayed on more deodorant
that stings her raw armpits, and finished
a load of laundry, bright white.
Now she holds her nails out to dry.
They are more red than the greasy
kiss around the lip of the empty cup.

Her other fingers drum the formica
while houseflies tap and ping off the glass
she washed squeaky clean. Some are caught
between the window and storm window.
Two are copulating there. A few more glint
dead, the size of pills, on the sill
she has not been able to touch for days.

History Lesson

If not for this century's
war to end all wars, America's
roaring Twenties crashing Depression,
threat of revolution, better
put all able-bodied poor
to work in factories just before
the Second World War, if not
for Appalachian hollow-dwellers
who lost hard-scrabble hillsides—
the rat takes the cheese, the bank
takes the farm, hi-ho the derry-o,
the bank takes the farm—
and rode the Hillbilly Highway North
to work in war plants where
they met and married their labors
to Slovenian immigrants washed ashore
after the above cited Great War,
I wouldn't even be here,
the son of cannon fodder
who survived the "police action"
in Korea with a purple heart
shrapnel legacy and heart-attacked
American dream. Books tell it like
history pivots from heroes.
I have what's called a good education.
There is a flag burning in my heart
like a monk on fire in Nam.

I Am Hiroshima

The horrible blossom
cultivated in the desert
of Jaweh's absolute law,
mushrooming Adam's
fallen brain driven
insane by the atom,
splitting it in a mania
of analysis to name
its power, to prove
a point, putting a gun
to his scientific head
because God is dead.

I am Hiroshima,
the flash that ate
so much innocent flesh,
the spark in the dark
of Oppenheimer's room
where time is running
out in a war to save
the world, ending
in a cradle of ash
glowing 20 thousand years.

I am Hiroshima
from the day I was born
until I am no more
bathed in the dawn
that balms the face
scorched by the firestorm,
the face I am trying
to make human again.

Cold Spring Walk

This cold, grey May rain
grips my tired spine.
The theme remains the same,
walk the talk till the grave.

Afternoons like this, the cusp
between Spring and Summer,
a drizzle falling cool
over warm earth smell rising,

I broke free of Catholic school
confines of thick, red brick rules
and scuffed down backstreets
under a canopy of new leaves.

No force of will can call
back now the one with all
I felt then but by following
the Holy Ghost to the source —

breathing through these bones
of words into pulse of deeds.

Tasting What of the Sun We Can

At the end of summer the last
of the tall grass stems yellow and hollow.
Rafts of ironweed and goldenrod
cluster over the field, and we both
recite their names, assuring each other.

We pick bristleberries that absorbed
their fill of the sun's pulses
and smash them between roof and tongue,
tasting what of the sun we can.
We spit—ripe is a day sooner than rotten.

I snap a black, fallen branch open
and smell the inside's incense
and hold the cherrywood out to you.
You draw in, then exhale, nodding good,
agreeing to what is passing.

Metamorphic

Lifting slabs of metamorphic rock
pressed and fused a long time ago
for a long time, I check underneath.

Worms recoil in coppery iridescence.
Beetles glint and burrow. Pale roots corkscrew.
Sowbugs, resembling small trilobites,

roll into balls, hiding their gills.
And eggs with their sparks, eggs
that I touch with my hand suddenly mortal.

Leafskeletons, bleached snail shells, bug husks—
stretched out on the forest floor too long,
I would become reduced to fine traces.

One respect I've learned, set the rock
back gently over the exposed ground
the way you found it. Close the door.

That Blue Spigot Handle

That blue spigot handle
down the basement dripping
as I try to fall asleep,
reminds of the encrusted one
found in the Chagrin flow,
an eight-spoked mandala
lesson of eternal turning,
reminds also of wagon wheel—
iron-belted wood—in a rut
at a western wear roadside
attraction where I stopped
to gas up and check the air
in right front, slow leak tire.
Squatting on hot pavement,
I stared down the wavering
all the way back to the first
paved road of the Minonians
at Knossos on the island of Crete.
Flagstones laid down millennium ago
joined the road that passed
the gift-shop and carried me back
here to this house where I rest—
but not before getting up
to shut off the water dripping.
The channels on the surface
of Mars were once thought to be
roads of a vanished civilization.
Now it's said, they carried water.

Fisherman Snagging Salmon on the Chagrin River

Coho and Chinock, stocked three years ago, are spawning now—
or trying to. They are two feet long and powerfully silver
to these weekend fisherman lined shoulder to shoulder
in rubber chest-waders. They tear through the green riffles
with lead weighted treble hooks below the fenced-in dam.
Huddled around the garbage drum's flames, we poke fun
at their seriousness and crowded determination.

As kids we used to wade the Chagrin every summer day we could,
soaked it in through our skin, and were familiar with its slow
carp, big as your thigh, their scales as coppery brown as pennies.
They would doze up and down stretches of sloughs over and over,
their big mouths unhinging and closing and opening again
to thoroughly vacuum up the foulest blooms of crawdad shell
and raw sewage hovering in the cool layers over the bottom.
We knew the oldtimers too, who got up earlier than us and caught
stringers of suckers to eat that flesh most said was all mud.

Once, down by the narrows, we watched a bowfisherman for
    an hour.
His reflection stood as poised and keen as a Great Blue Heron's.
Then the river was, for us, for a day, what it had been then
for the Erie people who understood hunger and hunting—
that killing was never only power, but blood taking blood.
They were sure to make prayer over the flashings of fish.

Pitching

for Huck Murray

We're back in your hometown this time,
but it could just as well be mine.
We're talking, picking up rocks and throwing
at fenceposts, telephone poles and mailboxes.
You pitch strikes 75% of the time—well,
maybe 50% —but you still have your form.
We both know, from practice, that to find
just the right stone, the right shape and weight,
is almost as important as the throw itself.
We each jiggle one around in our cupped hands
till it settles between our first two fingers,
then pick the heroes of the era we followed—
Seaver, Gibson, Palmer, or, if you could do
the dipsy-doodle windup and delivery, Louie Tiant—
and pitch three-quarters, overhand, side-arm strikes,
seeing them into the catcher's mit like you did
late nights upstairs listening to the Pirates out west.
I imitate Sudden Sam McDowell, the stalwart
of the woebegone Cleveland teams of the late sixties.
He only had a fastball, a hell of a fastball
when it wasn't wild, and a temper to match it.
But he taught me early lessons in a man's frailty:
maybe if he'd have stayed sober, he'd have pitched
his way out of some jams into the Hall of Fame.
And maybe, but for this break, or that bum elbow,
you'd be in the big leagues by now, Huck.
All afternoon we've walked and talked and thrown
our arms out, hitting, sometimes, pretty often,
the things we aimed at, the markers of home.

Tackling

Stan Zerucha, Ned Bindokas, Keith Zelazney, Chuck Dobish,
Jeff Marva, Woody Woodrow, Bill Uhaus, and Todd Plewacki.
Man, what a close music your names sound now,
coming to me here, far from Willoughby, like they are
the shouts and thuds and oomphs of backyard football.

Some of us listened to our uncles and went into computers.
Some pumped gas or moved furniture, or did the shifts
our fathers did at what factories were still burning nights.
Some remarried and moved back to the tract-house acres.
Some have a kid already, or kids, and Todd is dead.
None of us, as far as I know, go to Mass anymore.
None of us are born again, or really rich, or anything
terrible like that. I guess we're getting by somehow.

This evening after work, it becomes autumn again.
Walking to my room from a bar, I take in the crisp air
and it's as if I ran out for a long pass in the dusk
at the end of the vacant lot on Kilarney Drive.
I'm waiting for it to fall, standing there smelling
leaf-mulch, torn grass, and sweatshirts our mothers washed.
There's a rucus of tackling and laughing in the endzone.
You're all piling-on ontop of the loose ball
with that good feel of holding on to each other.

Evening Along the Chagrin River

A brown winter sparrow
clumps down beside
a stalk of sumac berries.

The juice-bright tongue
pierces the dusk
with 3...6...9 notes.

I bother up close
and alter the place
and singing altogether.

Clouds heavy and shift.
The river scours grey shale
a few calls downtrail.

I swing my curious
body backwards filling
the moment ago's space.

The first star appears,
one scale of a silver fish
drifted off elsewhere.

White-Tail Deer

I've come back to the fall banks
of the Chagrin river after years
of my life passed by unnoticed.

Around a bend, a deer startles out,
skids across a sheet of ice
and pokes through near the shore.

Crashing out, it bounds logs zigzag,
its white tail flashing and fading
into the darkening treeline.

A snowflake lights on the sleeve
of the plaid jacket I wore as a teen,
the spokes defined, then dissolved.

This Heron Is

Not a taoist painting,
though as still and able
to settle and fulfill
the space around itself.

Not the thought of the thing
I might have, painter's or
otherwise. That too, but more
than the quiet of brush strokes.

The heron itself
that waded here yesterday,
unperturbed, that stands still
after these words.

In the Heron's Heaving

In the heron's heaving burst
of blue wings and white breast,
the wading legs pull their length
from the dull pull of current
and the droplet speckled flash
washes fresh the sunlit willowleaves.

With a span of slender feathers
as long from tip to tip as
a boy is from head to muddy toes,
the heron's flight cleaves the haze,
loping up above the green
river carving walls of grey shale.

Staring at a Heron

August. Hazy. Midday.
I stand in the heron's stare,
the heron stands in this stare.
Neither of us will move.
Lulled to the same leisure
by the weather we share,
here we are each other.

The Chagrin River Watershed

Slate upon slate upon slate rippling
layers of riverbed the opaque snake of current contours,
uncoiling the valley.
Baked shale crumbles from grey cliff walls,
a chunk scatters down, startles across the surface
healing over, gliding on.
Invoking opening, Autumn sun intones
as hornet drones
through golden apple skin
as red-tail hawk circles azure sky
above leaf flourish brightness
that aches veins of eyes.

Perched on a red oak, root dangling overhang,
I plumb the Chagrin flow below—
the name thereof. Not from consterned shorthand
ascribed to English surveyor Cleaveland,
stymied by shallows and logjams,
but the anglicized pronunciation of "Saguin,"
French trapper who took to living the native way.
The first of his countrymen called it "Biche,"
"Elk," for Algonquin "Chin-noi-in-doh."
Herds laid off trails alongside, following the easiest grade
inland from the south shore of Great Lake migrations.
Longer than deer runs, their paths connected rivers,
were portages used by tribes and trappers.
Now they are the Ridge and River roads I drive
to arrive at this view,
cutting through forests once so thick
a squirrel could leap from Erie's shores to Ohio River,
never touching ground
unless flint-pointed down.

I grew up amid remnants of old growth
on the north ridge of an ancient inland sea.
As a boy I jumped off stranded dunes in a field
beside the house on the hill off Euclid Avenue
and found shells where once waves lapped—paved over now.
I learned time from the rings of cut pine
old man Robinson showed me in the backyard
of his World of Books house at the foot of Shankland Boulevard,
warming himself twice by cutting his own
as Thoreau advised.
South eastward from the Willoughby watertower,
I peered towards the foothills of Appalachia
from whence a line of my people came,
migrating until they hit the rusty lake and steel jobs.
Celts from glens, highlands and downs across the big pond,
they tried to stay one step ahead of industrial revolutions—
ending up again in mines when the land
fought or bought or stolen from the Shawnee
was sold out from under them by banks back east.
Their wood-lore passed across generations—
how to skin and cook a squirrel—was gradually dropped
for the convenience store on the corner.
Paradise keeps getting lost.

From this vantage I fly out
over New England style barns and a single clapboard spire
pointing above the maple-beech-oak-hemlock treeline,
out as far as the quarry-scarred side of Little Mountain,
glancing the alluvial outline of glaciers receding,
icicles dripping into foggy pools and wisps
swirling over mulchy bogs the first visitants found.
Moundbuilders, they hunted up from the Mississippi Valley,
sunflower seeds among their staples.
One can still see their faces.

Bobcat pelted Erie people camped on their remains,
carved owl-headed pipes for kinnickinick—
sumac leaves, inner bark of dogwood and nicotina rustica—
to induce dreams...of 60 acre shopping malls
and a multi-screen cineplex
encasing the last wetland hereabouts.

I strap sandals tighter, for a final wade before winter
hardens the Chagrin. The bones of my feet ache
as I pick my way through rapids
with a beaver-gnawed poplar staff,
past a head size stone in the flow
where five year old Jake reminded me I lost my face—
worn away by soft teeth of eternity's flow;
past also the brown-grey-beige bank of slate shards
where I layed down in the kiln of the sun
fossilized as a trilobite.
I come to the bouldery landfall
where rapids converge chutes and channels
into undertones and overflows, a fugue of currents
I hum as pulse percussing rivulets cleanse hearing.

Hiking back across elktrail-roadside field,
bumblebees nuzzling sluggish in wilting goldenrod cups,
I make my way up bridlepath hillside silence
to hemlocked gulleybrook. A woodthrush calls cluck-cluck-cluck
through hardwooded interior.
The last mosquitos hang hungry
in cold shafts of sunset.
Webs glister binding bare twig to curled, still green leaf.
A flicker works a beech trunk thunk-thunk.
Fox squirrels drop white oak husks.

A quorum of crows wheel the canopy, caw-cawing
a winter's advent scold.
Leaf-fall filled well-spring trickles black shale shelves,
watershed draining creek, river, lake, seaway, ocean to this revery.
The sky dilates, circles round this single blue-green-brown berry
suspended from a starry branch,
swallowed by the bird of night.

Postcard from Gullybrook

What's you hurry,
I tell my body
worrying the future.
There's only eternity
waiting up ahead,
a silence that will
snuff out this flickering
soon enough. So settle
back into forty winks
of the big sleep infused
with and grounded by
leaf, sun and shade,
delighted by dragonfly's
metallic delicacy hovering
above a bank of bluets,
mica glinting in sand
of shallows. This earth
is not lost, but merely
forgotten by way of highway's
hurtling progress above
Gullybrook's alluvial flow,
trickle of the ice-age
that assures these bones
will come rolling home,
scoured clean, wind's xylophone

In A Field Above the Freeway

The August sun lazes along.
Dull, yellow grasshoppers float
and collide from stem to stem.

On my break, hand propping my head,
I loll. The long weeds sway
and I just want to go with the flow.

But I have to head back down to work.
We're patching from here to Painesville.
I wave an orange flag, a single wing.

Standing, stretching my back to cracking,
I shift my weight, and the field
clutters outward in every direction.

Postcard from Middle America, Circa 1965

TV headed boy in tract-house project,
pseudo-suburban, wonderbread upbringing,
suckled on the blue-glow glass teat
along with frustrated mother's milk
laced with cessium 133 windborne
over the cow-grazing heartlands—
fallout from Uncle Sam's wargames
pictured mushrooming the tube
in 1959 Sciencefiction America.

He mutated to fit the situation.
Electro-chemical stimulus response
the bottom line—create a need
by burning a void into being
and filling it with all the things
money can buy, so when you grow up
you can sit in front of the TV,
eat chips, pop open a beer and
figure out what you want to watch.

Postcard from the Indiana Dunes

A flock of grey-white-black seagulls pegged one-legged,
facing wind, setting sun and rip-current
on a sandbar seventy miles due east
of Chicago's big shoulders floating
above Lake Michigan's horizon
like a latter-day Atlantis.

They do a yoga of wing stretching,
and settling webbed foot shaken back into foam,
keeping up their abulations
until they all turn and waddle
into tenacious hiss of beach grass—
two children walking in front of their father
coming into view, the cause of their move.

Chicago's gone in a cold, grey mist, and I watch
long white plumes from the smokestacks
of Gary on the extreme left, then
everything is gone—gulls, kids, Chicago—
and only an acrid stink lingers
and sand,
and waves,
and wind.

Postcard of a Farm Boy

To walk past,
present and future
in one step back
into his steps
the way the heart
dies forth, pausing
to see him, then see
through his eyes,
a farm boy tired
at day's end, weighted
by iron pegs hanging
from prongs of pitchfork
slung over suspendered
shoulders—to look
down through work
to soft, warm earth,
a stare of hard
wonder and animal
determination—
to sigh as wide
as sky and move through
other chores.

Postcard, Sunset, Louisville AFB

A pregnant Army transport taxies
around for take-off, rumbling
black-diesel over liquid asphalt.
It hulks up towards Kuwait
carrying tanks to protect oil.

Its drab desert-olive body banks
back and the smoke trail
cuts across the orange ball
of the sun like its the logo
of a doomed corporation.

But the sun just keeps sinking,
casting a hazy hue through
pollution, dying there
before and beyond anything
civilization can do about it.

Postcard from Motel Hell

Mangled flowers stuck in a beer bottle
outside her motel room door the morning after.
I ran into her as she padded the long hallway,
scrapping yellow and purple petals from slippers
into disinfectant reeking carpet. Her bathrobe slipped
from her pale, flabby varicose legs
that looked like stamped meat. "Where ya sleepin'?
You need a nightgown?" She asked, opening
for a free show, smiling
a winter rose chancre on her lip.

She was working that wing of the building
with her wheelchair-bound hubby,
getting what money and love she could
under his glare. I heard drunken truckers
playing cards in their room the night before,
pawing the spoils till she door slam sobbed
"I don't need nobody!" waking us each
to our own private motel hells.
She pounded her way back in an hour later.

That morning I had been down at the pool
tanning my ass, buffing up, contemplating
doing the minor-league strip club circuit—
better money than poetry or theater—
and here came the star of last night's show,
"Want a drink?" she continued, offering up
her coffee, non-dairy creme powder floating
the kahlua tinged styrofoam mouth of the cup.

She pulled it away, her grey toothed smile
turning sneer, "What are you afraid of?"
No denying that mirror we stared into,
flinching from whatever connection two souls,
locked out or lost, could possibly make.

Postcard from the Everglades

The Everglades don't look so "ever" anymore.
Stands of gaunt cypress and piney borders
wear an orange tinge—not a lazy sun color,
but the rusted shrivel of some chemical agent.
The grass sea chokes with man-induced mangroves
and oily effluent from sugar-cane processing.
The last in-bred panther stumbled down a culvert
near the Disney vortex and was turned hologram.
But you can see the heads of dozens of them
on the license plates of any traffic jam.
Behind the gates and the country club fountains,
the lawns of the condo development are as green
as new money, and the faces of dead presidents
are as pale as the legs of snowbirds in supermarkets.
No, the Everglades don't look so "ever" anymore.

Postcard from I-25 Wafflehouse

Alabama clear blue sky eyes
like the first cool day of fall
or first warm day of spring
walking out of stuffy highschool.
She's gumpop waitressing waffles
everyday for a year now, singing
every new country-western song
fresh off the jukebox til it ends
up under the plastic danish lid.
She hasn't taken to counting tips
or lines on her face like the lifers.
Stale afternoon coffee tastes bitter
but at least she still spits it out,
smiling in the teeth of nicotine sneers.

The Big Easy Sway

for Lee Grue and Shawn D. Jackson

The rusty sun barges westward up the Mississippi,
sinking swollen and woozy over the Quarter.
Started partying a little early and I peaked
too soon—hence this ballasted perspective from the edge
of the slow, bourbon whirlpool. Another reveler
tries to focus on what's left of a double hurricane
pink in its plastic souvenir cup, then starts doing
that open-container two-step stumble, pot-belly spilling
from his **"It's not the heat, it's the stupidity!"**
T-shirt, his face red as burled crawdad.

Nawlin's summer is a greasy sauna where smells take on shapes.
Presences of oyster-sloppy sexual decay hover corners,
mingling with etouffee ghosts, while stale beer
lingers down cool alleys mumbling to a memory
of patchouli that wafts by on a rare breeze stirring skirts
of Spanish moss, fanning fronds that exhale green
from between bricks mortared centuries before,
and insinuating through half-open shutters
to ruffle lacy interiors over rose-petal skin.

The Delta Swamp's fevered hands peel paint from shotgun shacks
in strips of stale pastry, in strips of ancient lingerie.
Her humid touch corrodes up floral, wrought iron trellises,
always ready to reclaim the dreams of her denizens
who simply push the bones of generations out
the back-hatches of cool, creole tombs and slide in
after one more night of hot, mystical incarnation—

all souls blowing their first and last breaths
through brassy jazz, handkerchiefs marching skyward.

I give a nod to Tennessee's panama-hatted pale shade
deep in a dry-rot wicker chair in an upper gallery.
Lids heavy, he gives a wry smile and toasts
his glass with inky hands, ice-cubes clinking into silence
as Lady Mississippi strolls over the levee,
her brown-golden bosom swelling and sighing
from her glittering evening dress cause
she ain't gonna follow no straight and narrow,
she's gonna roll her hips any which way she pleases,
the Big Easy swayin' through everybody she passes.

You, the Hoosier Poet, and the Ghost of Chinaski

for Ted Vaca

You drifted down here to heal in the Big Easy swirl,
expiating mistakes by getting as far down and out
as you can in your hole in the wall hell on crack corner.
You're not sure whether you're making a poultice
or drinking poison at this point, up all night cutting
Tarot, throwing ruins, and drawing down visions
of your daughter you crayon and tack on cracked plaster.

Your wake-up call is the late afternoon sun slanting through
the cataracted back-alley window as you wash down tabascoed
eggs with the last beer left in the empty fridge and walk to work.
Dusk seeps over the Quarter. The living and the dead spirits
and the tourists bump into you on your way down Bourbon Street
to the job at Marie Leveau's House of Voodoo dispensing trinkets
in the back room across from the glass-encased wax occultist.
You jot notes to your ex between customers with a glow-in-the-dark-
night-of-the-soul magic marker, trying to mend the wound of
        distance.

Then another drunk, then the bus back to your uptown flop where
every eight foot door wears a new padlock, but even that didn't stop
someone in the building from crowbarring the hinges off and stealing
your clock radio home-entertainment center and your underwear.
The Hoosier poet, kicked to the curb by his lover, is stone asleep
under the Chinaski Revolution fractured portrait left behind
by some other unfortunate doing their time in this purgatory.
He's trying to pawn the banjo on his knee to the tune of forty bucks
so he can get out of Dodge. Buk the spook lives down the hall like
the gatekeeper of lost desires. He does nothing for weeks until

melodrama rears its soap-operatic head and pitches a Scotch bottle
through the blaring TV. Echo of nothing again. Beer bottles cluster
around his door like toadstools tonight. Vomit haunts the hallways.

As if you needed a punctuation mark on that sign, Bob the dealer
comes pounding four in the morning on the door asking if you
    need
to put your stuff in some womens—been there, done that and
your daughter's picture hangs taped on a wall that has absorbed
countless come-cries, lost names, last testaments and dead beats.
You say the only thing that can keep you here after Mardi Gras
is death—keep a lid on that kind of mention in these climes.
A black cat sentence yowls in the courtyard below all night.
Love has such needle teeth when your heart is a scrap pulled out
from a stinking can spilled in the alley, and love devours everything.

I Was Unemployed In Phoenix Once, Then Spring Came

All winter it waited to release skyward.
Any body, any humming-by bird,
any insect, any dude would be stupid
not to get nose close to these blossoms
and partake of the apricot's whole business.

Meanwhile, there are people who wait in a line
that goes on too long, and the other line
moves faster, and their line might as well go west
like a broken-backed highway into the desert.
But nobody is going to lose their place in line.

By the hour, their feet are becoming more flat.
Blood at standstill, their mouths shut and stale.
To keep up, each one could use a cup of coffee.
This monotony is a purgatory
is what Washington calls 'the economy.'

Where the hell am I suppose to go—home—
so I can stare at the game show winner's grin,
the commercials showing me how clean
the house should be while I wait for them to give
me the check with all the zeros after my name.

There's a woman waiting in line downtown
getting more desperate by the minute who I'll join
sometime, and I'll tell her not to worry
about money. She'll tell me, "I gotta eat, don't I?"
Yes, but even so, the apricot blooms like crazy.

Love and Fear

Ya like that tattoo? They say there's no mistakes.
I can't even remember her face anymore
and her name is dyed there "4-Ever."
See this one, "L-O-V-E." See the other knuckles,
"F-E-A-R." Love and fear go hand in hand.
They're the two forces that motivate a man.
Well, me anyway. Can't speak for the rest.
I'm not exactly what you'd call the norm
Never have been norm. Never will be norm.
I stay outa that game. I stay on the road.
Not that truckin' is some kinda cakewalk.
A trooper back at the weigh station told me about a rig
they found idlin' out in the middle of the desert.
When they asked the driver what he thought he was doin',
he told'em, starin' straight ahead the whole time,
"I'm waitin' for the light to change.

Is it love or fear driven' me on? I love to drive
to some wide open space in the middle of the night,
pull over, pull out my sleepin' bag, lay flat on my back
and stare up at the stars as far as I can
til I hear crickets chirpin' in the clear mornin' air.
Get me a big sky plate of biscuits and gravy.
A hot cuppa mud warmin' the bones of my hands.
Happy to be here. Happy to be anywhere. And free.
Or is it fear? I'm not afraid to consider it—
some basic shark-like instinct keepin' me from stoppin'.
I spent some time in the can a while back
and believe me, it's been a motivator ever since.
Like they say, wherever you go, there you are.

Got 15 months for two joints of ditchweed.
I was stayin' with a woman up near Jerome.
The locals thought I was kinda an oddball
on account my bald head and Fu Manchu.
One mornin' I'm tryin' to get stoned on this oregano
when I see a commando jump over the back fence.
I thought I was hallucinatin' til I saw another one.
Next thing I know a swat team of sheriff's come
kickin' in the kitchen door, up the basement stairs,
through the bathroom window, down the chimney.
I never seen so many Federales—DEA, FBI, CNN.
They got a tip I had a kilo a Mexican in my rig.
You know what I was haulin'? Cheez-Wiz.
15 months in the Graybar Inn for two stinkin' joints.
Steal a little, you do the time.
Steal a lot, you're the man who sets the fine.

My cellmate was a real monster for tattoos.
He had this masterpiece stitched across his chest.
Not a professional job. Looked like he did it himself
with a ballpoint pen. On his right pec was a guy standin',
pointin'. On his left pec, right above where his heart
should be there's a guy kneelin'. I look closer
and the guy pointin' is holdin' a gun. And the kneelin' guy,
whose prayin' or beggin' for mercy, his brains
are gettin' blown all blue out the back of his head.
Underneath it there's this motto. I couldn't make it out
cause it was blurrin' into the fat of his gut,
so he reads it out loud for me, real slow-like.
"VIOLENCE', he says, "GETS THE JOB DONE." Then he smiles
his grey, jagged teeth and nods his shaved head.
15 months in the same cell with Mister Personality
will motivate ya to move and keep movin'.

Maybe I love fear. The danger out here on the edge.
Maybe I'm afraid of love. A soft bed I'll never leave.
Either way I drive right down the middle of it.
You're never sure which is which sometimes til it's too late.
Look at Elvis. All that adulation. End of his life
you know what he said? "I shoulda stayed a trucker."
Maybe he's still out here on the fringes of America,
floorin' a semi towards the gates of Graceland,
haulin' a load of velvet self-portraits.
Well, I'm gonna pull off up here in Barstow.
Remember this kid, whichever way you turn,
your ass is always behind you.

San Francisco

I saw San Francisco again this afternoon,
mumbling up on the edge of Free Park,
his hands fluttering out from the sleeves
of three greasy layers, preaching before
a mob of pigeons who want no words but bread,
their stomachs clenched around hunger.
His lost and found clothed brethren and
sistren scrounge the fringes for the offal
droppings from the sacred cash cow,
5 cents a can their sole redemption,
Alcatraz eyes drowning under the Bay sky.

One of them cleans the windshield of a limo,
black mirrored glass sliding up as it stretches by.
The vanity plate reads MAMMON, the Queen is in
a busy hurry for a meeting at the pyramid,
dealing disposable incomes, power-lunching
pie-charts, crunching numbers green as the bellies
of flies on dumpsters. She gives the thumbs down
from the vantage of her means-to-an-end domain.
One tap of her finger wipes out a thousand acres.
After cocktails, she will head down to the vault
to lay eggs—ptt, ptt, ptt—along the fault line.

But at those feet of clay, the Joshua-righteous
Invisible man raps on the doors of power,
the pulse of a man not addicted to the heads
of dead white men. And San Francisco continues
to sermon the pigeons hub-bubbing for goodies
from the broken pinata of civilization.
His rheumy eyes are stellar jays skipping through
redwood heights. His brown, wadded face spouts rapture,
and a swirl of black and grey bruises fly free.

The Dream Car We Drove West

At THE END of the way out west,
on the last two-laner
pinching into infinity,
There's a rusty red, white, and blue wagon
plowed into golden dust.
It's four doors hang
flung open to spacious skies.
The vinyl roof has been beat on
by the sun's fist
till it's as white as a cow's skull.
The engine's been picked clean
as a yokel's wallet.
Three of the tires were scrounged
long ago; the last is as flat
as a sharpie's five-dollar pork-pie hat.

An Indian-Head, buffaloed nickel
stays stuck between windshield
and dash, it's not enough
for a last call of the wild.
A yellowed Bible stolen
from a neon motel waits
to rise out of the glove box.
A garish brochure for Vegas
fades atop it. On the back seat,
bleached fried chicken bones
and empty beer cans rattle
with each 18 wheel gust.
A rabbit's foot dangles
from the cracked rear-window mirror
that stares all the way back
across us.

Where did they go, the dreamers?
Get-rich quick schemers,
guitar hero one-hit wonders,
soda-fountain starlets.
banjo-hitting bushleaguers
Ma an Pa five and dimers,
broken-down bronco busters,
fly-by-night storefront preachers,
hardscrabble migrant pickers
in the fields of paradise—
all the pilgrims.
Whoever hurried on
from this horse powerless hulk,
with their good looks, glad hands, fast talk,
and hunger for more,
whatever movie they ended up in,
they left more than what was left
of their innocence behind them,
driven on by the need to keep moving
and never look back.

Where has the pursuit of happiness
taken us?
Has the promised land ended
in the exhausted haze of Hell A?
Hollywood marketing Babylon
into redundant suburbs
trying so hard to be sane and clean
while the postman whistles
through clenched teeth,
murder staring up
from plastic wrapped papers

on doorsteps in tract house 'hoods
where gangstars shoot their own
action sequences segueing
from Rodeo Drive's parade of limos
while stemmers wither on skid row?
Where is our common ground America?
Built on a fault line?

As a I hitch-hiked Eastward, stranded
outside the city of Lost Angels,
on ol' Route 666,
across from the dream car we drove west
once upon a time,
I waited a long time for a ride
back home—wherever that is—
till a beat-up pick-up truck
driven by a long-hair
pulled over and popped open the door.
"Hop in," he says, "it's the Navajo way."

A Long, Long Way from Home

for T.J. Anderson

I think of you now stuck
in your room in the middle
of this great, white America
I could walk out of easy.

Hitchhiking once in the suburb
you call home, a cop pulled over
and asked you for your I.D..
"It's okay, he's one of our niggers."

This land is your land, Woody sang,
and a car company stole the tune
and put it brand new on the freeway
we keep escaping onto, to where?

Sometimes I feel like a motherless
child, a long, long way from home.
The poem of freedom is sold right out
from under us everyday, top dollar.

O Say Can You See?

O say can you see
this country free
of bigotry, hostility, and incivility
from sea to shining tee-vee?

The tribes are picking up sides
from Bosnia to Belfast to LA
and there's nowhere left to hide
for the children of the dream
walking hand in hand
down the black and white wound
running across this land.

What's wrong with this picture?
Can you find the human
being beaten on this screen?
Being beaten on **this** screen?
He deserved it. Payback happens.
What goes around, comes around
said the eye for an eye blind men.
But the rioting **is** on the wall.
Mr. President, you have a call
on the white courtesy phone.

"It's the BLANKS fault. The BLANKS
started it. You know how they are."
"They don't really belong here."
So we sell ourselves on talk-shows
like bugs shaken in a jar.
And the finger of blame points around
in an angry trigger circle.

We're all living in the same hood now,
buying into Babylonian hype.
Mad. Ave. went to bed with Holly Would,
raised a little family of stereotypes.

Hey, can you see
somebody looks just like me,
somebody looks just like me,
peering out from the leaves
of your family tree
rooted in Mother Africa?
We are the children of the dream
who wandered our separate ways
a long time gone, gathered together
here again today. Remember?
Can we call ourselves sisters? Brothers?

What color was the hand
raised against Abel
after it fell? How will we ever
wipe the slate clean
when the powers that be
sell us whitewash and
sell us spray-paint
so we can paint ourselves
into our own little corners,

the mirrors of our monsters?
Can you see the eyes
of a sister and brother, mother and father,
behind the masks of your worst nightmares?

O say can you see
through the lies that we are not us?
That we are always us-versus?
And where is Justice? Or is it Just Us?

We are the children of the dream
wandering the desert
of America through the smoke
from the fire next time come,
walking hand in hand
down the black and white wound
running across this land
healed over with each step
together—O say can you see
the person walking next to you?

Buddy-Ray Mac

(to the tune of "Little Red-haired Boy")

I am a gypsy poet and rhymnin's what I do
from Beantown to San Fran all the way to Tuscaloo;
I'm known from Chicago to Nawlins and back
and they call me by the name of Buddy-Ray Mac.

Of all the jobs I could do, poetry's the best,
for when I get tired I just shut up...and rest;
I can sing for my supper, what else is there to do
but wander the world singing news of the muse.

So it's do ci do and around we go
and where we stop well God only knows.
Love leads to life, life leads to death,
it's the circle of sound til we draw our last breath.

Well I'm heading down the road in a beat-up car,
and if I make it home I'll thank my lucky star;
Need some dough-ray-me or I'll fall-so-low,
keep me off your couch with a little cash flow.

I sing of life's joy, I sing of life's pain,
and in the end they balance out the same.
Now you've heard some stories from Buddy-Ray Mac,
May Spirit bless and keep you til I come back.

About the Author

Ray "Buddy" McNiece is a poet, playwright, actor, singer, and teacher, of Appalachian Irish and Cleveland Slovenian heritage. He follows the footsteps of endless other gypsy poets, once travelling over 40,000 road miles in a year long tour. He has performed around the country in the burgeoning performance poetry circuit and abroad in Greece, Spain, France, Germany, England, Scotland, and recently at the opening of City Lights in Florence, Italy. In 1999 he was chosen National Poetry Slam Champ.

McNiece is the author of two previous books of poems and monologues: *Dis—Voices from a Shelter* and *The Bone Orchard Conga.* He has written and performed two solo theatre works of monologues, poems and songs including *Dis* and *US? Talking Across America.* With Shawn D. Jackson he co-authored *Conversations: Homegirl Meets Whiteboy,* a satirical deconstruction of American stereotypes.

The author is a satellite member of Alternate Roots, a progressive Theatre Alliance. He performs and leads performance and writing workshops through his educational theatre company, Page to Stage Productions. He often performs two character based shows in the schools, *Johnny Applesed* and *The Seanachie*, a program of Irish stories, songs, and poems.

Ray was the founder of the Writers League of Boston and has been a captain of two National Poetry Slam Championship teams, Boston in 1992 and Cleveland in 1994. He lives near Cleveland, Ohio, and performs with the poetry/music project Tongue-in-Groove.

"I am blessed to be following my bliss. I give thanks to the creator, to ancestors for guiding me on the way, and to all those people and places that inspired these words. May the poem rise to meet you..."

My Homepage: **http://members.aol.com/raymcniece**